MY JOURNAL

My name is ....

and I am .... years old.

Hi There! If you enjoyed this book, please don't forget to leave a review on Amazon. Just a simple review will help us out a lot. Thank you!

Family

DATE: . . . .

Today is: (Monday) (Tuesday) (Wednesday) (Thursday) (Friday) (Saturday) (Sunday)

How big is your family? Why is that a good size, or not such a good size?

☆ I used capital letters.   ☆ I used spaces.   ☆ I used punctuation.

Family

DATE: . . . .

Today is: (Monday) (Tuesday) (Wednesday) (Thursday) (Friday) (Saturday) (Sunday)

What are the good things about being the youngest child in a family?

☆ I used capital letters.   ☆ I used spaces.   ☆ I used punctuation.

Family

DATE: . . . .

Today is: (Monday) (Tuesday) (Wednesday) (Thursday) (Friday) (Saturday) (Sunday)

What are the bad things about being the youngest child in a family?

☆ I used capital letters.　　☆ I used spaces.　　☆ I used punctuation.

Family

Today is: (Monday) (Tuesday) (Wednesday) (Thursday) (Friday) (Saturday) (Sunday)

What are the good things about being the oldest child in a family?

☆ I used capital letters.   ☆ I used spaces.   ☆ I used punctuation.

Family

Today is: (Monday) (Tuesday) (Wednesday) (Thursday) (Friday) (Saturday) (Sunday)

What are the bad things about being the oldest child in a family?

☆ I used capital letters.   ☆ I used spaces.   ☆ I used punctuation.

Family

DATE: . . . .

Today is: (Monday) (Tuesday) (Wednesday) (Thursday) (Friday) (Saturday) (Sunday)

How much time do you spend with grandparents?

☆ I used capital letters.   ☆ I used spaces.   ☆ I used punctuation.

Family

DATE: . . . .

Today is: (Monday) (Tuesday) (Wednesday) (Thursday) (Friday) (Saturday) (Sunday)

What is the best number of children to have in a family? Why?

☆ I used capital letters.   ☆ I used spaces.   ☆ I used punctuation.

Family

DATE: . . . .

Today is: (Monday) (Tuesday) (Wednesday) (Thursday) (Friday) (Saturday) (Sunday)

What can older brothers and sisters do to help with younger brothers and sisters?

☆ I used capital letters.   ☆ I used spaces.   ☆ I used punctuation.

Pets

DATE: . . . .

Today is: (Monday) (Tuesday) (Wednesday) (Thursday) (Friday) (Saturday) (Sunday)

What is the best kind of pet, and why?

☆ I used capital letters.   ☆ I used spaces.   ☆ I used punctuation.

Pets

Today is: (Monday) (Tuesday) (Wednesday) (Thursday) (Friday) (Saturday) (Sunday)

What is better, a home with a pet or a home without a pet?

☆ I used capital letters.   ☆ I used spaces.   ☆ I used punctuation.

Pets

DATE: . . . .

Today is: (Monday) (Tuesday) (Wednesday) (Thursday) (Friday) (Saturday) (Sunday)

You really want a pet, but your parents say you have to choose between an enormous spider and an enormous snake. Which do you choose, and why?

☆ I used capital letters.　　☆ I used spaces.　　☆ I used punctuation.

Pets

DATE: . . . .

Today is: (Monday) (Tuesday) (Wednesday) (Thursday) (Friday) (Saturday) (Sunday)

What are the good things about having a pet rabbit?

☆ I used capital letters.   ☆ I used spaces.   ☆ I used punctuation.

Pets

DATE: . . . .

Today is: (Monday) (Tuesday) (Wednesday) (Thursday) (Friday) (Saturday) (Sunday)

What are the bad things about having a pet rabbit?

☆ I used capital letters.   ☆ I used spaces.   ☆ I used punctuation.

Home

DATE: . . . .

Today is: (Monday) (Tuesday) (Wednesday) (Thursday) (Friday) (Saturday) (Sunday)

Does the size of your house matter? Why / why not?

☆ I used capital letters.　　☆ I used spaces.　　☆ I used punctuation.

Home

DATE: . . . .

Today is: (Monday) (Tuesday) (Wednesday) (Thursday) (Friday) (Saturday) (Sunday)

Do you think sharing a bedroom with a brother or sister is a good idea or a bad idea? Explain.

☆ I used capital letters.　　☆ I used spaces.　　☆ I used punctuation.

Home

Today is: (Monday) (Tuesday) (Wednesday) (Thursday) (Friday) (Saturday) (Sunday)

What's the best floor to live on in an apartment building? Why?

☆ I used capital letters.   ☆ I used spaces.   ☆ I used punctuation.

Home

Today is: (Monday) (Tuesday) (Wednesday) (Thursday) (Friday) (Saturday) (Sunday)

What chores do you do?

☆ I used capital letters.   ☆ I used spaces.   ☆ I used punctuation.

Home

DATE: . . . .

Today is: (Monday) (Tuesday) (Wednesday) (Thursday) (Friday) (Saturday) (Sunday)

Do you think you do the right number of chores? Why / why not?

 I used capital letters.   ☆ I used spaces.   ☆ I used punctuation.

Home

DATE: . . . .

Today is: (Monday) (Tuesday) (Wednesday) (Thursday) (Friday) (Saturday) (Sunday)

Who does most of the chores in your family? Why?

☆ I used capital letters.   ☆ I used spaces.   ☆ I used punctuation.

Home

DATE: . . . .

Today is: (Monday) (Tuesday) (Wednesday) (Thursday) (Friday) (Saturday) (Sunday)

Do you think girls and boys should do the same chores or different chores? Why?

☆ I used capital letters.　　☆ I used spaces.　　☆ I used punctuation.

Home

DATE: . . . .

Today is: (Monday) (Tuesday) (Wednesday) (Thursday) (Friday) (Saturday) (Sunday)

Is there anything you want to do that your parents won't let you do? What is it?

 I used capital letters.   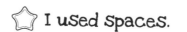 I used spaces.   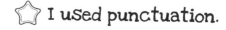 I used punctuation.

Home

DATE: . . . .

Today is: (Monday) (Tuesday) (Wednesday) (Thursday) (Friday) (Saturday) (Sunday)

If you have children when you grow up, will you treat them the same way your parents treat you, or will you treat them differently? If differently, then how?

☆ I used capital letters.　　☆ I used spaces.　　☆ I used punctuation.

Home

DATE: . . . .

Today is: (Monday) (Tuesday) (Wednesday) (Thursday) (Friday) (Saturday) (Sunday)

Do your parents give you an allowance? How much?

 I used capital letters.   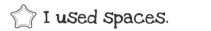 I used spaces.   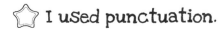 I used punctuation.

Home

DATE: . . . .

Today is: (Monday) (Tuesday) (Wednesday) (Thursday) (Friday) (Saturday) (Sunday)

What kind of allowance should a child of your age get?

☆ I used capital letters.   ☆ I used spaces.   ☆ I used punctuation.

Home

Today is: (Monday) (Tuesday) (Wednesday) (Thursday) (Friday) (Saturday) (Sunday)

Should a child be expected to work for their allowance? How much work is fair?

⭐ I used capital letters.   ⭐ I used spaces.   ⭐ I used punctuation.

Home

Today is: (Monday) (Tuesday) (Wednesday) (Thursday) (Friday) (Saturday) (Sunday)

Could your family manage without a car? How?

☆ I used capital letters.   ☆ I used spaces.   ☆ I used punctuation.

DATE: . . . .

Today is: (Monday) (Tuesday) (Wednesday) (Thursday) (Friday) (Saturday) (Sunday)

How big is your family? Why is that a good size, or not such a good size?

☆ I used capital letters.   ☆ I used spaces.   ☆ I used punctuation.

Today is: (Monday) (Tuesday) (Wednesday) (Thursday) (Friday) (Saturday) (Sunday)

How big is your family? Why is that a good size, or not such a good size?

☆ I used capital letters.   ☆ I used spaces.   ☆ I used punctuation.

DATE: . . . .

Today is: (Monday) (Tuesday) (Wednesday) (Thursday) (Friday) (Saturday) (Sunday)

How big is your family? Why is that a good size, or not such a good size?

☆ I used capital letters.   ☆ I used spaces.   ☆ I used punctuation.

Today is: (Monday) (Tuesday) (Wednesday) (Thursday) (Friday) (Saturday) (Sunday)

How big is your family? Why is that a good size, or not such a good size?

☆ I used capital letters.   ☆ I used spaces.   ☆ I used punctuation.

Birthdays

DATE: . . . .

Today is: (Monday) (Tuesday) (Wednesday) (Thursday) (Friday) (Saturday) (Sunday)

Write a sentence about the best birthday party you've ever been to.

 I used capital letters.   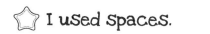 I used spaces.   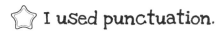 I used punctuation.

Birthdays

DATE: . . . .

Today is: (Monday) (Tuesday) (Wednesday) (Thursday) (Friday) (Saturday) (Sunday)

What do you want to do for your next birthday?

 ☆ I used capital letters.   ☆ I used spaces.   ☆ I used punctuation.

Birthdays

DATE: . . . .

Today is: (Monday) (Tuesday) (Wednesday) (Thursday) (Friday) (Saturday) (Sunday)

If you could choose only one gift for your next birthday, what would it be?

☆ I used capital letters.   ☆ I used spaces.   ☆ I used punctuation.

School

DATE: . . . .

Today is: (Monday) (Tuesday) (Wednesday) (Thursday) (Friday) (Saturday) (Sunday)

Should school be fun or serious? Why?

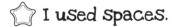 I used capital letters.   ☆ I used spaces.   ☆ I used punctuation.

School

Today is: (Monday) (Tuesday) (Wednesday) (Thursday) (Friday) (Saturday) (Sunday)

What is a good teacher like?

☆ I used capital letters.   ☆ I used spaces.   ☆ I used punctuation.

School

DATE: . . . .

Today is: (Monday) (Tuesday) (Wednesday) (Thursday) (Friday) (Saturday) (Sunday)

What is a bad teacher like?

☆ I used capital letters.   ☆ I used spaces.   ☆ I used punctuation.

School

DATE: . . . .

Today is: (Monday) (Tuesday) (Wednesday) (Thursday) (Friday) (Saturday) (Sunday)

Does school start too early? What time would you like it to start, and why?

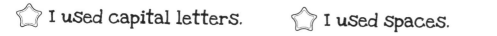 I used capital letters.   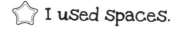 I used spaces.   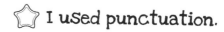 I used punctuation.

School

DATE: . . . .

Today is: (Monday) (Tuesday) (Wednesday) (Thursday) (Friday) (Saturday) (Sunday)

How much homework do you get?

☆ I used capital letters.　　☆ I used spaces.　　☆ I used punctuation.

School

DATE: . . . .

Today is: (Monday) (Tuesday) (Wednesday) (Thursday) (Friday) (Saturday) (Sunday)

Do you think children should get homework? Why/Why not?

☆ I used capital letters.   ☆ I used spaces.   ☆ I used punctuation.

School

DATE: . . . .

Today is: (Monday) (Tuesday) (Wednesday) (Thursday) (Friday) (Saturday) (Sunday)

Do you think children who bully other children should be punished? If you do, then how should they be punished?

☆ I used capital letters.   ☆ I used spaces.   ☆ I used punctuation.

School

DATE: . . . .

Today is: (Monday) (Tuesday) (Wednesday) (Thursday) (Friday) (Saturday) (Sunday)

What is your favorite subject and why?

☆ I used capital letters.   ☆ I used spaces.   ☆ I used punctuation.

School

DATE: . . . .

Today is: (Monday) (Tuesday) (Wednesday) (Thursday) (Friday) (Saturday) (Sunday)

How can teachers help a child who finds schoolwork difficult?

☆ I used capital letters.   ☆ I used spaces.   ☆ I used punctuation.

School

DATE: . . . .

Today is: (Monday) (Tuesday) (Wednesday) (Thursday) (Friday) (Saturday) (Sunday)

What do your parents do to help you do well at school?

 I used capital letters.   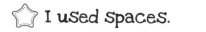 I used spaces.   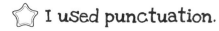 I used punctuation.

Friends

DATE: . . . .

Today is: (Monday) (Tuesday) (Wednesday) (Thursday) (Friday) (Saturday) (Sunday)

What are the most important qualities in a friend?

☆ I used capital letters.   ☆ I used spaces.   ☆ I used punctuation.

Friends

DATE: . . . .

Today is: (Monday) (Tuesday) (Wednesday) (Thursday) (Friday) (Saturday) (Sunday)

How long have you known your oldest friend?

☆ I used capital letters.   ☆ I used spaces.   ☆ I used punctuation.

Friends

DATE: . . . .

Today is: (Monday) (Tuesday) (Wednesday) (Thursday) (Friday) (Saturday) (Sunday)

What do your friends like about you?

☆ I used capital letters.   ☆ I used spaces.   ☆ I used punctuation.

Friends

DATE: . . . .

Today is: (Monday) (Tuesday) (Wednesday) (Thursday) (Friday) (Saturday) (Sunday)

What do your friends not like about you?

 I used capital letters.   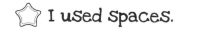 I used spaces.   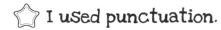 I used punctuation.

Activities

DATE: . . . .

Today is: (Monday) (Tuesday) (Wednesday) (Thursday) (Friday) (Saturday) (Sunday)

When you're not at school, how much time do you spend outdoors?

☆ I used capital letters.   ☆ I used spaces.   ☆ I used punctuation.

Activities

DATE: . . . .

Today is: (Monday) (Tuesday) (Wednesday) (Thursday) (Friday) (Saturday) (Sunday)

How much time do you spend watching television? Is that too much time?

☆ I used capital letters.   ☆ I used spaces.   ☆ I used punctuation.

Activities

DATE: . . . .

Today is: (Monday) (Tuesday) (Wednesday) (Thursday) (Friday) (Saturday) (Sunday)

Do you think that playing video games is a waste of time? Explain your opinion.

☆ I used capital letters.   ☆ I used spaces.   ☆ I used punctuation.

Activities

DATE: . . . .

Today is: (Monday) (Tuesday) (Wednesday) (Thursday) (Friday) (Saturday) (Sunday)

What is your favorite kind of book?

 I used capital letters.    I used spaces.   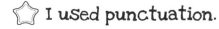 I used punctuation.

Activities

DATE: . . . .

Today is: (Monday) (Tuesday) (Wednesday) (Thursday) (Friday) (Saturday) (Sunday)

Would you rather read a book or watch a movie? Why?

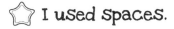 I used capital letters.   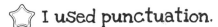 I used spaces.   I used punctuation.

Activities

DATE: . . . .

Today is: (Monday) (Tuesday) (Wednesday) (Thursday) (Friday) (Saturday) (Sunday)

What is your favorite movie, and why?

☆ I used capital letters.   ☆ I used spaces.   ☆ I used punctuation.

Activities

DATE: . . . .

Today is: (Monday) (Tuesday) (Wednesday) (Thursday) (Friday) (Saturday) (Sunday)

What is your favorite movie about?

☆ I used capital letters.   ☆ I used spaces.   ☆ I used punctuation.

Activities

DATE: . . . .

Today is: (Monday) (Tuesday) (Wednesday) (Thursday) (Friday) (Saturday) (Sunday)

How many times have you watched your favorite movie?

 I used capital letters.    I used spaces.   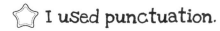 I used punctuation.

Activities

DATE: . . . .

Today is: (Monday) (Tuesday) (Wednesday) (Thursday) (Friday) (Saturday) (Sunday)

Which sport is more fun, baseball or football? Why?

☆ I used capital letters.   ☆ I used spaces.   ☆ I used punctuation.

Activities

Today is: (Monday) (Tuesday) (Wednesday) (Thursday) (Friday) (Saturday) (Sunday)

Which is more fun, swimming or running? Why?

☆ I used capital letters.   ☆ I used spaces.   ☆ I used punctuation.

Activities

DATE: . . . .

Today is: (Monday) (Tuesday) (Wednesday) (Thursday) (Friday) (Saturday) (Sunday)

Do you have a hobby? Did you choose it or did your parents choose it?

 I used capital letters.   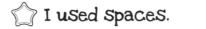 I used spaces.   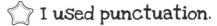 I used punctuation.

Activities

DATE: . . . .

Today is: (Monday) (Tuesday) (Wednesday) (Thursday) (Friday) (Saturday) (Sunday)

What's good about your hobby?

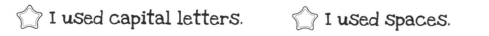 I used capital letters.   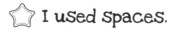 I used spaces.   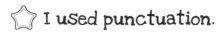 I used punctuation.

Activities

DATE: . . . .

Today is: (Monday) (Tuesday) (Wednesday) (Thursday) (Friday) (Saturday) (Sunday)

What's bad about your hobby?

☆ I used capital letters.   ☆ I used spaces.   ☆ I used punctuation.

Activities

DATE: . . . .

Today is: (Monday) (Tuesday) (Wednesday) (Thursday) (Friday) (Saturday) (Sunday)

What is the most dangerous sport you know? Why is it dangerous?

☆ I used capital letters.   ☆ I used spaces.   ☆ I used punctuation.

Activities

DATE: . . . .

Today is: (Monday) (Tuesday) (Wednesday) (Thursday) (Friday) (Saturday) (Sunday)

What's the best picture you've ever painted?

☆ I used capital letters.   ☆ I used spaces.   ☆ I used punctuation.

Activities

DATE: . . . .

Today is: (Monday) (Tuesday) (Wednesday) (Thursday) (Friday) (Saturday) (Sunday)

It's your mum's birthday and you have no money to buy her a present. What can you make for her?

☆ I used capital letters.   ☆ I used spaces.   ☆ I used punctuation.

Holidays

DATE: . . . .

Today is: (Monday) (Tuesday) (Wednesday) (Thursday) (Friday) (Saturday) (Sunday)

Would you rather go camping or stay in a hotel? Why?

☆ I used capital letters.　　☆ I used spaces.　　☆ I used punctuation.

Holidays

DATE: . . . .

Today is: (Monday) (Tuesday) (Wednesday) (Thursday) (Friday) (Saturday) (Sunday)

What is the most fun thing about going camping?

☆ I used capital letters.   ☆ I used spaces.   ☆ I used punctuation.

Holidays

DATE: . . . .

Today is: (Monday) (Tuesday) (Wednesday) (Thursday) (Friday) (Saturday) (Sunday)

What is the worst thing about going camping?

☆ I used capital letters.   ☆ I used spaces.   ☆ I used punctuation.

Holidays

DATE: . . . .

Today is: (Monday) (Tuesday) (Wednesday) (Thursday) (Friday) (Saturday) (Sunday)

What is the best thing about staying in a hotel?

_____

- -

_____

- -

_____

- -

_____

- -

_____

- -

_____

 I used capital letters.    I used spaces.   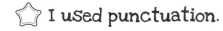 I used punctuation.

Holidays

DATE: . . . .

Today is: (Monday) (Tuesday) (Wednesday) (Thursday) (Friday) (Saturday) (Sunday)

What is the worst thing about staying in a hotel?

☆ I used capital letters.   ☆ I used spaces.   ☆ I used punctuation.

Holidays

DATE: . . . .

Today is: (Monday) (Tuesday) (Wednesday) (Thursday) (Friday) (Saturday) (Sunday)

Would you rather spend your holidays at home or go away?

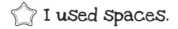 I used capital letters.　　　⭐ I used spaces.　　　⭐ I used punctuation.

Holidays

DATE: . . . .

Today is: (Monday) (Tuesday) (Wednesday) (Thursday) (Friday) (Saturday) (Sunday)

If you could go on holiday anywhere in the world, where would you go and why?

☆ I used capital letters.   ☆ I used spaces.   ☆ I used punctuation.

Holidays

DATE: . . . .

Today is: (Monday) (Tuesday) (Wednesday) (Thursday) (Friday) (Saturday) (Sunday)

If you could do anything you wanted on holiday, what would you do?

☆ I used capital letters.   ☆ I used spaces.   ☆ I used punctuation.

Holidays

DATE: . . . .

Today is: (Monday) (Tuesday) (Wednesday) (Thursday) (Friday) (Saturday) (Sunday)

Would you rather spend your holiday with your family or with your best friend? Why?

☆ I used capital letters.   ☆ I used spaces.   ☆ I used punctuation.

Holidays

DATE: . . . .

Today is: (Monday) (Tuesday) (Wednesday) (Thursday) (Friday) (Saturday) (Sunday)

Is going to camp a good experience or a bad one? Why?

☆ I used capital letters.　　☆ I used spaces.　　☆ I used punctuation.

Holidays

DATE: . . . .

Today is: (Monday) (Tuesday) (Wednesday) (Thursday) (Friday) (Saturday) (Sunday)

Is the summer break too long or too short? How long should it be?

☆ I used capital letters.   ☆ I used spaces.   ☆ I used punctuation.

Holidays

DATE: . . . .

Today is: (Monday) (Tuesday) (Wednesday) (Thursday) (Friday) (Saturday) (Sunday)

What's better and why – Thanksgiving or Christmas?

 ☆ I used capital letters. ☆ I used spaces. ☆ I used punctuation.

Holidays

DATE: . . . .

Today is: (Monday) (Tuesday) (Wednesday) (Thursday) (Friday) (Saturday) (Sunday)

What do you think of Santa?

☆ I used capital letters.   ☆ I used spaces.   ☆ I used punctuation.

Holidays

DATE: . . . .

Today is: (Monday) (Tuesday) (Wednesday) (Thursday) (Friday) (Saturday) (Sunday)

Do you give your parents Christmas presents?

☆ I used capital letters.   ☆ I used spaces.   ☆ I used punctuation.

Holidays

DATE: . . . .

Today is: (Monday) (Tuesday) (Wednesday) (Thursday) (Friday) (Saturday) (Sunday)

What's the best present to give someone your age?

☆ I used capital letters.   ☆ I used spaces.   ☆ I used punctuation.

Holidays

DATE: . . . .

Today is: (Monday) (Tuesday) (Wednesday) (Thursday) (Friday) (Saturday) (Sunday)

You're going away on holiday for two weeks. You're allowed to take clothes and one other thing. What do you take?

☆ I used capital letters.   ☆ I used spaces.   ☆ I used punctuation.

Time

DATE: . . . .

Today is: (Monday) (Tuesday) (Wednesday) (Thursday) (Friday) (Saturday) (Sunday)

What is your favorite season? Why?

☆ I used capital letters.   ☆ I used spaces.   ☆ I used punctuation.

Time

DATE: . . . .

Today is: (Monday) (Tuesday) (Wednesday) (Thursday) (Friday) (Saturday) (Sunday)

What is your least favorite season? Why?

 I used capital letters.    I used spaces.   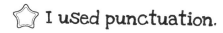 I used punctuation.

Time

DATE: . . . .

Today is: (Monday) (Tuesday) (Wednesday) (Thursday) (Friday) (Saturday) (Sunday)

What time do you get up on Tuesdays? Why?

☆ I used capital letters.   ☆ I used spaces.   ☆ I used punctuation.

Time

DATE: . . . .

Today is: (Monday) (Tuesday) (Wednesday) (Thursday) (Friday) (Saturday) (Sunday)

What time do you get up on Sundays? Why?

 I used capital letters.    I used spaces.   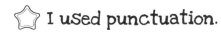 I used punctuation.

Time

DATE: . . . .

Today is: (Monday) (Tuesday) (Wednesday) (Thursday) (Friday) (Saturday) (Sunday)

Do you get enough sleep? If not, then why not?

☆ I used capital letters.   ☆ I used spaces.   ☆ I used punctuation.

Time

DATE: . . . .

Today is: (Monday) (Tuesday) (Wednesday) (Thursday) (Friday) (Saturday) (Sunday)

How much sleep does a child of your age need?

_____

- -

_____

_____

- -

_____

_____

- -

_____

_____

- -

_____

 I used capital letters.   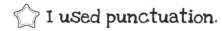 I used spaces.   I used punctuation.

Time

Today is: (Monday) (Tuesday) (Wednesday) (Thursday) (Friday) (Saturday) (Sunday)

How much sleep does an adult need?

☆ I used capital letters.   ☆ I used spaces.   ☆ I used punctuation.

Time

DATE: . . . .

Today is: (Monday) (Tuesday) (Wednesday) (Thursday) (Friday) (Saturday) (Sunday)

How old do you think you'll be when you get your first job?

☆ I used capital letters.   ☆ I used spaces.   ☆ I used punctuation.

Time

DATE: . . . .

Today is: (Monday) (Tuesday) (Wednesday) (Thursday) (Friday) (Saturday) (Sunday)

How old do you think you'll be when you retire (stop working)?

☆ I used capital letters.　　☆ I used spaces.　　☆ I used punctuation.

The Future

Today is: (Monday) (Tuesday) (Wednesday) (Thursday) (Friday) (Saturday) (Sunday)

What's the perfect age to be? Why?

☆ I used capital letters.   ☆ I used spaces.   ☆ I used punctuation.

The Future

DATE: . . . .

Today is: (Monday) (Tuesday) (Wednesday) (Thursday) (Friday) (Saturday) (Sunday)

What kind of job do you want to do when you grow up?

☆ I used capital letters.　　☆ I used spaces.　　☆ I used punctuation.

The Future

DATE: . . . .

Today is: (Monday) (Tuesday) (Wednesday) (Thursday) (Friday) (Saturday) (Sunday)

Do you want to have children when you grow up? Why/why not?

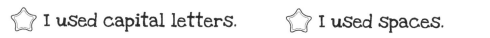 I used capital letters. 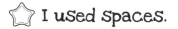 I used spaces. 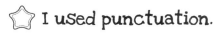 I used punctuation.

The Future

Today is: (Monday) (Tuesday) (Wednesday) (Thursday) (Friday) (Saturday) (Sunday)

Do you think being an adult is better or worse than being a child? Why?

☆ I used capital letters.   ☆ I used spaces.   ☆ I used punctuation.

The Future

DATE: . . . .

Today is: (Monday) (Tuesday) (Wednesday) (Thursday) (Friday) (Saturday) (Sunday)

What's harder work, going to school or going to work?

☆ I used capital letters.   ☆ I used spaces.   ☆ I used punctuation.

The Future

DATE: ....

Today is: (Monday) (Tuesday) (Wednesday) (Thursday) (Friday) (Saturday) (Sunday)

What are you looking forward to doing as an adult that you can't do as a child?

☆ I used capital letters.　　☆ I used spaces.　　☆ I used punctuation.

The Future

DATE: . . . .

Today is: (Monday) (Tuesday) (Wednesday) (Thursday) (Friday) (Saturday) (Sunday)

Would you like to do your dad's job? Why/why not?

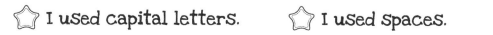 I used capital letters.  I used spaces. 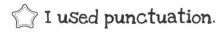 I used punctuation.

The Future

Today is: (Monday) (Tuesday) (Wednesday) (Thursday) (Friday) (Saturday) (Sunday)

Would you like to do your mum's job? Why/why not?

☆ I used capital letters.   ☆ I used spaces.   ☆ I used punctuation.

The Future

DATE: . . . .

Today is: (Monday) (Tuesday) (Wednesday) (Thursday) (Friday) (Saturday) (Sunday)

What's more important — having an interesting job, or having a job that pays lots of money? Why?

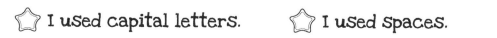 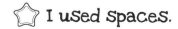

The Future

DATE: . . . .

Today is: (Monday) (Tuesday) (Wednesday) (Thursday) (Friday) (Saturday) (Sunday)

If you had lots of money, would you still get a job? Why/Why not?

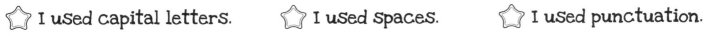 I used capital letters.    I used spaces.   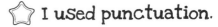 I used punctuation.

Superpowers

Today is: (Monday) (Tuesday) (Wednesday) (Thursday) (Friday) (Saturday) (Sunday)

Choose two superpowers.

 I used capital letters.  I used spaces. 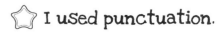 I used punctuation.

Superpowers

Today is: (Monday) (Tuesday) (Wednesday) (Thursday) (Friday) (Saturday) (Sunday)

What's the best superpower, and why?

☆ I used capital letters.　　☆ I used spaces.　　☆ I used punctuation.

DATE: . . . .

Superpowers

Today is: (Monday) (Tuesday) (Wednesday) (Thursday) (Friday) (Saturday) (Sunday)

Which of these superpowers do you choose, and why — being able to walk on water OR being able to run twice as fast as anyone else in the world?

 I used capital letters.   I used spaces.   I used punctuation.

Superpowers

Today is: (Monday) (Tuesday) (Wednesday) (Thursday) (Friday) (Saturday) (Sunday)

Who is the best superhero, and why?

☆ I used capital letters.   ☆ I used spaces.   ☆ I used punctuation.

Superpowers

Today is: (Monday) (Tuesday) (Wednesday) (Thursday) (Friday) (Saturday) (Sunday)

In a fight between Batman and Spiderman, who would win, and why?

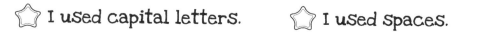 I used capital letters.  I used spaces. 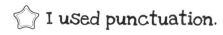 I used punctuation.

Superpowers

Today is: (Monday) (Tuesday) (Wednesday) (Thursday) (Friday) (Saturday) (Sunday)

You can choose to communicate with one kind of animal. Which animal do you choose, and why?

☆ I used capital letters.   ☆ I used spaces.   ☆ I used punctuation.

SAVE THE LITTLE PIG

Bonus

Bamboo Modern Press
Want More Books:
Available at amazon

Made in the USA
Las Vegas, NV
24 March 2023

69592600R00059